Introducti

Real ITSM

Rob England

(The IT Skeptic)

Sensible business practices

© Two Hills Ltd 2008

Created by Two Hills

letterbox@twohills.co.nz

www.twohills.co.nz

PO Box 57-150, Mana
Porirua 5247
New Zealand

Published by Lulu
First published 2008
ISBN 978-1-4092-2300-9

This book is for those who work in Information Technology (IT) and for those who have IT done to them.

Service Management is all the rage in IT at the moment, hence "ITSM". The leading description of ITSM is ITIL®.

This book is not about ITIL. Really. Real ITSM™ is a tongue-in-cheek satirical look at what the real-life practices might be, as compared to the idealised models in frameworks like ITIL or COBIT or ISO20000 or ...

In the tradition of "real ale", Real ITSM is the genuine thing as it is found on the streets, not the sanitised commercial offerings marketed to the masses.

Through humour we can explore some of the disconnects between the idealised framework and its actualisation in the dysfunctional cultures so common in real ITSM.

About the author

The IT Skeptic is the pseudonym of Rob England, an IT consultant and commentator. He has twenty years experience mapping business requirements to IT solutions, ten of them in service management. He is active in the itSMF (the professional body for IT Service Management). He is the author of a popular blog at www.itskeptic.org and many articles taking a critical look at IT's absurdities, especially those relating to ITIL and CMDB. He is also a paid-up Skeptic. He lives with his wife and son in a small house in a small village in a small country far away.

Cover photo by the author: the cutting edge nerve-centre on Level 3 of Two Hills World Headquarters Tower.

The mug can be purchased at http://www.itskeptic.org/shop.

```
┌─────────────────────────────────┐
│ ┌─────────────────────────────┐ │
│ │                             │ │
│ │      The Real ITSM          │ │
│ │     community is at         │ │
│ │   www.realitsm.com          │ │
│ │                             │ │
│ └─────────────────────────────┘ │
└─────────────────────────────────┘
```

Dedicated to Brian Johnson and Paul Wilkinson who pioneered ITSM humour (if there can be such a thing).

Contents

Foreword

An English joke goes along the lines that a pilot landing a plane in New Zealand announces in his welcome message that passengers should reset their watches by putting them back fifty years.

Well, they never met Rob England who in my opinion (which with $3.85 will buy you a café latte here in Noo Yawk), is a good few years ahead of the rest when it comes to IT service management controversies. Or should I say discussion points.

When reading the book, I was (along with Paul Wilkinson) flattered to see the dedication in this satire with regard to us being the pioneers in putting the humour into ITSM, IhumourTSM, we called it. It did not catch on.

Then I noticed that in the index my name appears just above the entry for 'known idiot'. I hope that doesn't catch on either.

And rather than spoil the fun by abstracting the jokes, instead I will spoil the certification process by providing the answers to the 'hard' questions in the new exams; these are;

> Q1; yes
>
> Q5; only when the wife/husband/life entity is absent
>
> Q14; who says?
>
> Q27; because in the final print run, Satanists managed to inscribe texts in the annexes that led to outsourcing.

I always wanted to do that.

And in closing these useless remarks to a book that made me laugh out loud, I reckon Rob may need to find a tin hat to wear for a while because his satire hits the mark rather too often and rather too accurately.

Brian Johnson
Author of some ITIL stuff

Preface

Like all bad ideas, this one started out small and just grew. Originally this was going to be a small book run quickly through the on-demand publishing system to learn some of the pitfalls before publishing That Which Comes After, The Book About ITIL. That way I would only make new mistakes on the second book.

But this book developed a life of its own, with a related website (www.realitsm.com) and a club (EgoITSM), and silly illustrations.

A word about those illustrations: there is a story that Neil Young only played guitar and never sang because he was too embarrassed about his voice, until one day he heard Bob Dylan. I felt the same way about my drawing when I saw Scott Adams' *Dilbert*. Unfortunately, Neil Young sings better than I draw.

This book has been a lot of fun to write, and I hope it is a lot of fun for you to read, and to join in to the Real ITSM world. Welcome.

Some thanks are in order at this point:

To the reviewers Terry Barwick, Charles Betz, Lyndon Christie, Val England, Brian Johnson, and Paul Wilkinson.

To all the people who labour so hard to create ITIL and COBIT and ISO20000 to give me something to take pot shots at.

Most of all to Vee and Jack for patiently leaving me alone in my office.

Thank-you.

Rob England
Pukerua Bay
August 2008

1
Introduction

IT operational theory is all very well for those who have the luxury of time and money.

But what do you do if systems are in flames, users are openly hostile, budgets are falling, staff morale is a mess, and the CIO role is career death?

You apply Real ITSM. This is the only operational framework that recognises how IT is delivered in the real world and then adapts itself to minimise the impact on that environment while maximising the value to those who have to deliver it.

Low cost, low impact, easy and quick — Real ITSM is the preferred framework for most of today's IT departments, making IT Real.

Get Real.

1.1 What is Real ITSM?

Real ITSM is a Body of Knowledge (BOK). This means Real ITSM collects together all the ideas, good and bad, new and old, as a compendium of knowledge for ITSM practitioners.

Real ITSM is a framework for implementation, which means it represents proven and generally accepted Real ITSM practices.

Real ITSM represents the leading edge in Real ITSM thinking, providing thought leadership to the industry and ensuring that it will remain fresh for years to come.

The fact that there is a fundamental contradiction between these three statements has not escaped us, but it doesn't seem to trouble ITIL so we won't let it distract us either.

These are early days for Real ITSM. What you hold is Real ITSM 1.0 but we are confident that Real ITSM will grow to be a BOK more hyped than ITIL, more rigorous than COBIT, more useful than MOF, more boring than PMBOK, and more misunderstood than CMMI.

Unlike all these other BOKs, Real ITSM does not represent best practice or good practice or generally accepted practice or even worst practice.

Real ITSM represents Real Practice: ITSM as it is done in the real world[1].

---

[1] Real Practice has some similarities with Core Practice, a.k.a. CoPr, another bright idea of the author's. Core Practice is the minimum necessary to get the job done without raising risk above some threshold. See www.corepractice.org Real ITSM has no connection, affiliation or similarity with the legal product Real Practice™ at www.realpractice.com. Real ITSM has nothing to do with the law and prefers to keep it that way.

1.2   *Principles of Real ITSM*

Anyone who has experienced the contented tranquillity of a mature and stable IT organisation will long for such a work environment.

Such a pleasant place to work is achievable with some commitment and the rigorous application of Real ITSM principles, known as Realitsm and pronounced **ree**-uh-litz-m, near enough to "realism".

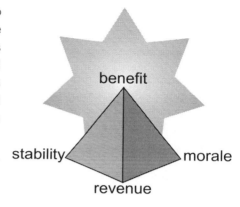

Figure 1-1   Realitsm

The main threats to IT stability are change, accountability and reduced spending. Realitsm is about eliminating these threats from the IT environment, in the best interests of all in IT. A harmonious IT environment requires adherence to the following Realitsm principles:

- Ensure a stable operating environment

- Maximise adaptability to change

- Promote involvement through collectivist decision-making

- Maintain morale through reduced group accountability

- Maximise revenue and funding for the IT department

- Maximise benefit and value for the IT staff

1.3   *Real ITSM vs. ITIL*

ITIL presents "best practice"[1], an idealised model for us all to aspire to. ITIL is all very well for theorists, academics, consultants and IT managers, and all others similarly detached from reality.

Down here in the real world, at the coalface, an entirely different model prevails: Real ITSM, which represents Real Practice.

Real ITSM involves its own lifecycle, activities, roles and metrics, analogous to those of ITIL but entirely different. They differ because, unlike ITIL, they must engage with the real, physical world, populated by "wetware" - those cussed, unpredictable and generally useless devices known as People.

When any idealised model meets People, the laws of logic are suspended, and rationality flies out the window.

Figure 1-2   ITIL vs. Real ITSM

When ITSM frameworks go through this realitsm transformation, the output is Real ITSM. Most BOKs are process-centric. Real ITSM is people-centric: it understands that what really happens is dependent on the people – their motivations, culture, personal agendas, fears and desires.

---

[1] **ITIL Version 3 wimped out to "good practice"**

1.4 Aligning IT with the business

This concept is very much in vogue. In fact it is already so, like, you know, 2005, and the new thing is "integrating IT with the business" which is really new and exciting and different.

Figure 1-3 Realitsm: IT united

This is of course nonsense. IT is a part of the business, except where it has been outsourced but those businesses won't be around too long so we can disregard them here.

We don't get worked up about aligning Distribution with the business or integrating Finance. IT is just another department and ought to behave like one; that is, it should act to protect its own vested interests and expand its empire.

Take a look at the Human Resources department of any organisation. Or Marketing. Nobody could seriously suggest these departments act in the interests of the greater organisation. Nor should IT. If it did, it just might find itself out of business.

IT is supposedly becoming a commodity (famously argued by Nicholas Carr's "*IT Doesn't Matter*"). Organisations don't have an Electricity department. IT might be absorbed by Building Services. Nobody in IT wants to end up wearing a grey lab-coat or using pencils, so IT must work assiduously to avoid this fate.

United IT stands, integrated it falls.

1.5   Real ITSM model

Real ITSM consists of

- a Deathcycle which follows a service from misconception to abandonment

- a set of Activities performed

- related Roles to be put on wetware's business cards and otherwise ignored

- Metrics used to distort behaviours

- Complimentary Guidance

Unlike ITIL, which uses the word "process" with a cavalier disregard for any generally accepted definition of the word, Real ITSM prefers to refer to "activities". We do this partly because it is a better-suited word and partly to keep the OGC lawyers at bay. This does mean that the "four Ps"

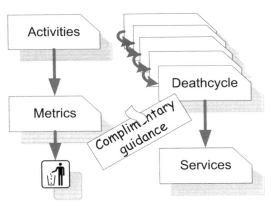

Figure 1-4 Real ITSM model

doesn't work any more (People Processes Products Partners), so Real ITSM uses the alternate model of Wetware Activities Stuff and Parasites which is just as mnemonic: WASP.

Real ITSM activities are carried on in all Deathcycle phases independent of services. The Deathcycle is, like, just a model, you know. Real activities carry on regardless.

1.6 *Deathcycle*

Real ITSM services go through a Deathcycle from misconception to a usually messy end. Navigating the ITSM Deathcycle can be thought of as akin to navigating the Great Barrier Reef. The intent of Real ITSM is to minimise the number of services that actually go live, while maximising the time and education of staff along the way.

In the event that a service does reach the users, the opposite focus prevails: it should be kept alive for as long as possible so as to maximise revenue and job assurance. The intent however is the same – minimisation of change.

The Deathcycle is made up of five areas or domains or sections or stages or phases:

Service Reaction	Planning and strategy is forbidden. All Real ITSM acts in reaction to business pressures.
Service Demand	Services are created only in concession to the demands of the customers.
Service Taming	Services arrive unexpected and unannounced. First priority is to get some control over them.
Service Nursing	Once stuck with a service, the focus is on keeping it alive as long as possible to maximise revenue.
Continual Service Assessment	Management, consultants and staff are kept happily occupied measuring and assessing the services.

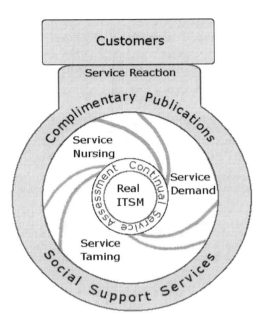

Figure 1-5 Real ITSM

1.7 *Value proposition*

The reason that ITIL projects can be so expensive and drawn out is that the model ITIL imposes is so different from the reality of business-as-usual. Because Real ITSM is much more closely mapped to current realities, Real ITSM can be implemented quickly with very little cost.

This creates the secondary spin-off benefit that change is minimised. Real ITSM implementations cause far less disruption than ITIL, have less impact on staff morale, and generate less staff turnover.

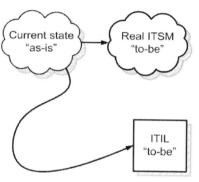

Change is equally unsettling to end-users. It is reassuring for them to see IT delivering as it has always done even after a Real ITSM implementation project.

Nevertheless, Real ITSM formalises the existing organisation. This allows management to attend retreats and workshops; change job titles;

Figure 1-6 Close mapping

rearrange organisational structures and reporting lines; and issue large quantities of documentation, posters and emails. This makes them happy and keeps them out of the working staff's hair while they concentrate on running the organisation.

Finally the Real IT Service Institute™ or RITSI plans to hold annual conferences in Cancun, Bali and Monaco which benefits everyone involved.

1.8 Organisation

Real ITSM is represented by the Real IT Service Institute, or RITSI. The Institute is incorporated in London[1]. Membership is inclusive: open to all vendors, consultants, trainers, examiners and publishers without exception (unless we don't like you).

The RITSI Board of Directors is elected by the RITSI Board of Directors. Nominations are open to anyone who we tell. In order to serve its international constituency, the Board meets in resorts worldwide.

RITSI and its agents do derive revenues from Real ITSM, but this income is used solely to fund the cost of operations, the ongoing enhancement and promotion of Real Practice, and the financial viability of the various organisations.

RITSI operates a number of programs for the benefit of the Real ITSM community[2].

1.8.1 CultITSM

CultITSM is RITSI's program of promotion and marketing of Real ITSM, and in particular the website, newsletters, events, RITSI products and the products and services of RITSI members (especially those members who sponsor or advertise with RITSI, or who manage to finagle a place on the Board).

Vendors welcome the opportunity to promote their industry using subscription fees and volunteer labour. RITSI and CultITSM provide the mechanism.

---

[1] London, Tanzania not London, England
[2] The Real ITSM community is of course the vendors, consultants, trainers, examiners and publishers.

1.8.2   BAPITSM

Business And Professional ITSM is a registration program for Real ITSM practitioners. For a small fee, Real ITSM professionals can become full accredited members of the RITSI.

Membership is subject to review and approval of the Institute, and is restricted to only those who have paid the fee.

Ongoing accreditation is maintained by demonstrating experience in Real ITSM and a regular program of professional development, such as attending Real ITSM webcasts, courses and meetings.

1.8.3   EgoITSM

For those too tight or disreputable for BAPITSM, there is EgoITSM, an open register of Real ITSM practitioners.

Anyone may register (remarkably there is no fee), and gain access to the EgoITSM forum, discounts, and the lovely **Cult**ITSM newsletter.

Since RITSI does not validate this information or confirm the authenticity of the identity, and we do not recommend, warrant or guarantee their services in any way, explicit or implied (remember they are Real practitioners!), the value of registering is questionable but it can certainly do no harm other than to the reputation of the registrant.

One tangible benefit is the ability to print off a nice meaningless certificate.

1.8.4   PragmaITSM[1]

Everybody understands that students at training courses retain less than a quarter of what they learned, and that classroom learning is an order of magnitude less effective than practical application.

Therefore Real ITSM only requires classroom training courses from those willing to pay for them. Remaining training is done on the more pragmatic basis of the PragmaITSM program, where Real ITSM practitioners demonstrate experience by the rigorous process of saying so. For a small fee, this experience is reviewed by the PragmaITSM accreditation agency and the candidate's qualification is certified.

See also *Real ITSM Qualifications*, page 19.

1.8.5   FavorITSM

In order to regulate the Real ITSM industry, and thereby protect the integrity of RITSI and public confidence in Real ITSM, RITSI issues compliance certification to users, products, and services under the FavorITSM[2] program.

Other frameworks have sadly neglected the revenue potential of such compliance certification, and have left it open to foraging commercial entities. RITSI has no intention of making the same mistake, although for a suitable consideration from an interested party we could conceivably reconsider this policy.

See *Real ITSM Compliance,* page 17, for details.

---

[1] PragmaITSM has no connection, affiliation or similarity with the nice company pragmITSM at www.pragmitsm.com. Antipodean brains think alike. Real ITSM has nothing to do with selling software and prefers to keep it that way.
[2] Yes the American spelling. Real ITSM generally uses spelling from the inventors of the language, but in this case it looks nicer.

1.8.6 ParasITSM

RITSI understands the beneficial symbiosis between an industry and its analysts. The more analysts invest in understanding something, the more interested they are in promoting it to ensure future return on their investment by selling that expertise. Therefore the ParasITSM program provides support for analysts, such as:

- Crash introductions to Real ITSM, usually over lunch, known as "Talk the Talk"

- References customers representative of the happy customer base

- Recognised industry experts available for interview

- Boilerplate text for white papers, guaranteed unique and untraceable

- List of vendors willing to be reviewed, and a table of recommended charges

- Keynote slots at all conferences

1.8.7 DogmaITSM

The integrity of the Real Practice content is of course paramount to RITSI. The Institute retains a part-time unqualified career bureaucrat to govern the ongoing development of that content through the DogmaITSM program.

DogmaITSM keeps the core content up to the state of the art through reviews every seven to ten years. It employs a commercial tendering process to find the most knowledgeable authors. To ensure Real ITSM's relevance to the whole world, authors must be selected from vendors from more than one country. See also *Contributing to Real ITSM*, page 23.

In addition the DogmaITSM program certifies Real Complimentary Guidance, see page 22.

1.8.8   DespoITSM

Like similar closed non-public-domain BOKs, Real ITSM is copyrighted and trademarked. RITSI protects its intellectual property rigorously, policed by the DespoITSM program.

The Program (as it is known, as in "Oh no! Not The Program!" [dramatic chord]) enforces:

- Misuse of copyright material

- Violation of trademark

- Parody and satirical mockery of Real ITSM

- Unpaid bills

- Overdue subscriptions

- Overdue books from the RITSI Library

Enforcement is outsourced to Lou and Stan's Debt Collections and Intellectual Property Enforcement Inc. Lou and Stan have an uncanny ability to avoid drawn-out legal arguments and a remarkable number of affiliates in other countries.

1.9   *Real ITSM royalty*

There is no governance in ITSM (though it creates some data for governors to use).   There is no governance in IT (though it also creates data for its masters).   Governance is performed by governors, who don't work in IT (heck governors don't *work*).   So we have no need to discuss governance in Real ITSM, except for the issue of who governs the Real ITSM BOK community.

Now that "management" has come to mean anything that people do, and "governance" is used to mean what "management" was supposed to, this raises the small problem of what to call Real ITSM governance.   So Real ITSM refers to reigning and sovereignty instead.   [Note: there will be an issue when the King takes out the garbage, and managers are known as "gods".   What is next?]

Real ITSM has no ultimate ruler, per se.   Real ITSM has the following royalty:

- RITSI Chairman of the Board (Rob England)

- RITSI CEO (Rob England)

- DogmaITSM Chief Architect (Rob England)

- PragmaITSM Chief Examiner (Rob England)

- FavorITSM Chief Assessor (Rob England)

- Webmaster (Rob England)

- Accreditation Agency (Two Hills Ltd: Rob England, CEO)

You can see that Real ITSM has devolved authority across a number of sovereign roles to ensure a balance of powers.

1.10 Assessment

Since Real ITSM does not actually change anything, the bulk of practitioner activity will be directed at assessing the current state. As this will be the only source of income for consultants it is proposed that assessment will be performed monthly until either funds dry up or the consultant retires (see *Continual Service Assessment*, page 71).

The wording of Real ITSM practices is vague enough to make measurement straightforward (see *Real ITSM Compliance*, page 17).

At the end of relevant sections of this book, you will find a table to assess your own current state. Go to the RITSI website at www.realitsm.com to download these as an assessment spreadsheet of Real Practice and to compare your score with that of other Real ITSM sites.

1.10.1 Maturity Model

The Real ITSM Maturity Model is based on the CMM[1].

The optimum maturity level is level 1, although level 0 is acceptable. Since Real ITSM is modelled on the real world, all Real ITSM activities usually exist (level 1).

If an IT department chooses to eliminate the activity (move to Level 0) in the interests of simplicity and a quiet life, this is usually a sensible decision.

And since resistance to change, flexibility in the face of inevitable change, and lack of accountability are essential elements of Real ITSM, attempts to move activities to other maturity levels are seen as counter-productive and result in corrective action.

---

[1] CMM is the Carnegie Mellon Model, later renamed as the Capability Maturity Model, now known as CMMI, which has been a significant revenue and recognition generator for Carnegie Mellon ever since the US defense industry paid for its development. It is very successful because it is very useful.

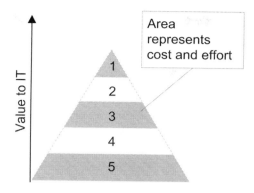

Area represents cost and effort

Figure 1-7   Real ITSM maturity

1.11 Compliance

Unlike some other frameworks, Real ITSM does not overlook the opportunity, and of course the importance, of certifying organisational and product compliance to Real ITSM.

It is frequently stated that loosely worded frameworks such as Real ITSM or ITIL are too vague and too open to interpretation to serve as the basis for compliance certification.

Simple consideration of the problem shows the error in this reasoning.   Such degrees of freedom make it easier to assess compliance, not harder.

So the RITSI's FavorITSM program will, for a small fee, issue Real ITSM compliance certification to any product, organisation or individual who

- Has the money

- Assures the Institute that they are compliant

RITSI recognises that in some circumstances these strict criteria might unreasonably restrict an entity's ability to achieve certification, so Real ITSM certification follows the ISO 20000 model by allowing candidates to define the scope within which their offering is to be considered for compliance.

So for example a company could seek compliance within just one country. Or a consultant could seek compliance for just their suit and shoes rather than their whole service.

Certified entities are expected to always specify the scope of certification when referring to their certificate. Actually we expect you never will but "expected" is a nice cop-out word to say it is not our fault when you don't.

In order to facilitate this process, a compliance spreadsheet is available on the website at www.realitsm.com with the "yes" responses helpfully defaulted. The submission mechanism and payment details can be found there too, as well as a public database of accredited entities.

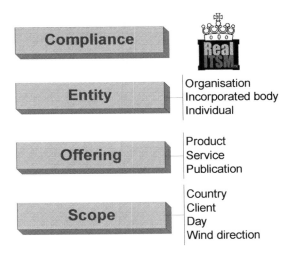

Figure 1-8 Real ITSM Compliance Certification Model

No organisation may conduct certified compliance assessments, or offer alternate Real ITSM compliance certification schemes without accreditation, for a not so small fee, from RITSI[1].

---

[1] Note: as the official accreditation agency for the RITSI, all fees are paid to Two Hills Ltd.

1.12 Qualifications

Some time in the future the PragmaTSM program will assemble the Council of Real ITSM Matriculation Examiners (CRIME) to develop a PragmaTSM certification program in conjunction with all those who stand to profit most from it (this being the standard industry approach).

The main activity to certify is assessment. There will also be activities around consultation, requirements gathering, reorganisation, tool selection, documentation, recommendation, review and other similar essential activities.

The proposed Real ITSM Qualification Scheme has four levels:

- Fundament (also known as Sheep-dip)

- Interpretive ("what Real ITSM really means is...")

- Expert

- Real Expert

For a small additional fee, successful candidates will receive a certificate printed on genuine leather-effect paper, and a coloured lapel badge. The colours will be changed on a rotational basis every five years.

The Real ITSM qualification scheme and examinations are set by the RITSI's official PragmaTSM accreditation agency Two Hills Ltd in close consultation with Two Hills Ltd.

In the best interests of the trainees, training courses are limited to no more than 30 trainees per instructor, except for online courses where there is no limit. Courses must last at least the prescribed period (generally three hours) except where agreed by a majority of the trainees.

Training courses and examinations can only be delivered under licence from Two Hills Ltd, who will, for a fee, accredit an Endless Income (EI) or Annuity Training Opportunity (ATO).

The Real ITSM Qualification Scheme is clearly illustrated in Figure 1-9.

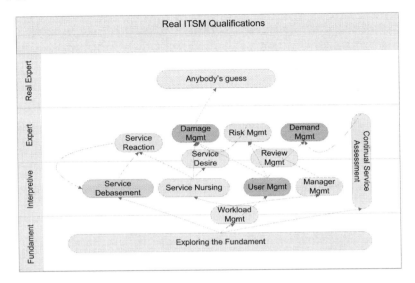

Figure 1-9   Real ITSM Qualification Scheme

Note how the structure follows Bloom's Taxonomy of Learning[1].

Fundament candidates are immediately equipped on graduation to participate meaningfully in decision-making workshops for their organisation's ITSM projects or to deliver the same training professionally to others.

As candidates pass each of the Interpretive modules, they can confidently be relied on to design processes, manage teams, and as the name implies interpret the Real ITSM wisdom into something adapted to their own organisation, based on their prejudices, biases and whims.

Once a candidate achieves Expert status, they will be transformed overnight into an expert able to advise corporations on the strategy and design of multi-million dollar ITSM project or manage those same projects to an assured successful completion.

---

[1] Oh it's some system of stuff that has four levels and we have four levels so that's close enough to "following".

So important, and magical, is the transformation into ITSM Expert that all graduations are to be performed in an initiation ceremony. Each ATO is free to design their own initiation, so long as it includes secret signs, table-tennis paddles and chickens.

The Qualification scheme for the highest level of all - Real Expert - has not been agreed yet, nor may it ever be as it is unlikely to be economic for anyone to achieve it.

Ascending into Real Expert status can only be achieved by either (a) transcending mortal form or (b) being one of the old boys in the inner circle before the qualification was announced.

Unlike many other frameworks, Real ITSM qualification certifications are published on a central PragmaITSM database at www.realitsm.com.

Real ITSM certification is far too valuable a qualification to allow anyone to fraudulently claim they have achieved it. This would be unfair to those who work so hard to earn it legitimately (especially after going through the initiation ceremony).

Note: an alternative PragmaITSM path to qualification is provided to those with extensive practical experience in the Real ITSM industry who may, for a small fee, apply to the RITSI's accreditation agency for "grandfathering clause" certification. We look after our old mates.

1.13 Complimentary Guidance

External third-party books that say nice things about Real ITSM may apply to be accredited by RITSI's DogmaITSM program as Real Complimentary Guidance.

For a small administrative fee they will be linked to from www.realitsm.com and mentioned endlessly in books and presentations.

The following guidance has already been certified as complimentary to Real ITSM:

- Real Value Learning Systems www.realvaluelearning.com

- Harry's Hot Autos www.onlydroveonsundays.com

- The Bulgarian Institute of Horizontal Folkdance www.LovelyBulgarianGirls.com

For the latest list see www.realitsm.com/DogmaITSM

In addition to Complimentary Guidance, the following frameworks have synergy with[1] Real ITSM:

- ITSM From Hell

- COBIT

- CMMI

- ISO/IEC 20000

- ISO/IEC 15504

- ISO/IEC 10995:2008

- Oh alright… ITIL

---

[1] **We don't know what it means either**

1.14 Contributing to Real ITSM

There are four ways to contribute to Real ITSM:

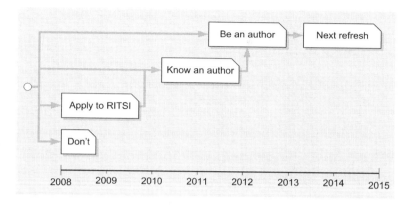

Figure 1-10   Contribute to Real ITSM

1. Be an author. Wait seven years for the next Real ITSM Refresh. Tender for one of the books. Be one of about a dozen people worldwide to win a tender. Devote a year of your life to writing a book.

2. Know an author. Get networking now: you have seven years to guess who the next ones will be and get into their professional circle. Then persuade them your idea is better than theirs.

3. Contact the RITSI DogmaITSM program to tell them you have some content to contribute. There is no documented process to do this, not any advertised contact point, but RITSI are bureaucrats so you should find them helpful and communicative. Once you have their attention, they will put you in touch with the next authors. See 2 above.

4. Forget it.

Note: organisations or individuals who feel passionately that certain content should be included in Real ITSM can appeal to the RITSI's Official Architect, Two Hills Ltd, who will, for a small fee, incorporate content in the next edition.

Real fish

2
Service
Reaction

The modern world is entirely too dynamic for any sort of medium or long term planning to be worthwhile.

Governments, laws, executives, competitors, technologies, recessions and fads come and go like the weather. As the old military saying goes "No plan survives the first encounter". Strategic planning is as futile as an umbrella in a cyclone. Real ITSM understands this and prohibits all strategic planning as an irresponsible waste of resources. Better to sail the unpredictable winds of change, as flexible and unencumbered as possible.

2.1 Service Reaction principles

Unlike ITIL Version 3 which has introduced a strategic practice, Real ITSM is entirely reactive. Like ITIL's Version 3 *Service Strategy*, Service Reaction is esoteric and best not approached first (starting ITIL with *Service Strategy* can result in permanent injury). Work on the other four domains of the Deathcycle first so as to be sufficiently numb to deal with Service Reaction.

Service Reaction describes basic Realitsm principles.

- Determine the maximum practical forecast period MPFP, usually six months. Limit all financial planning to the MPFP. Note that budgetary planning is exempt from the MPFP: it can project as far as a full year. But no more. All subsequent years in a budget should be entirely hypothetical, if not downright fictional.

- Under-utilise all key resources, in order to provide emergency capacity for executive whims, budget cuts, mass layoffs, mergers and similar blind-side events. This includes staff, computer servers, networks, budgets, disk storage…

- As a corollary, prohibit all optimisation, efficiency or consolidation activities.

- Document only a very few procedures (usually just enough to pass the ISO9000 audit) and enforce none of them. Repeated procedures ingrain habit, which stifles staff creativity and flexibility. The more different ways a procedure is performed, the higher the probability that one of those ways will still work after cataclysmic change. This is simple Darwinism[1]. Repeatable processes are like the agricultural monoculture of a cloned crop: highly productive in good times but highly vulnerable to disease, pests, climatic extremes or other stresses.

- Dampen all feedback. Any engineer will tell you that an undamped feedback system can oscillate dangerously.

---

[1] Few mutations are positive, but that is the price we pay.

Therefore all reports and metrics should provide only enough information to support the allocation of blame, and must contain sufficient time-lag to prevent runaway feedback loops. Remove any unnecessary transparency.

- Prohibit continual improvement. Once a system is barely adequate, leave it alone. Its life expectancy is short so why invest in optimising something that will be torn down soon enough? Any Real change that does happen is to be based on the Wright[1] Cycle of Guess-Do-Crash-Fix.

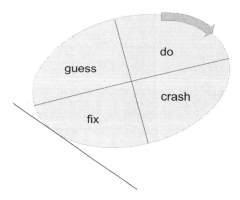

Figure 2-1 The Wright Cycle

- Stamp out grass-roots initiatives. Management are almost certainly planning something in secret that will render the staff initiative pointless, usually when the investment is at a maximum and the returns not yet realised.

- Create initiatives only in response to an executive directive. Invest the minimum necessary to prevent punishment. This will be just enough to make excuses possible, and considerably less than that necessary to effect[2] any progress. This is called the Law of Conservation of Investment and is illustrated by a three colour Venn diagram thingy in a university text somewhere.

---

[1] Named for the Wright Brothers, who crashed many an airplane before they got one off the ground.

[2] No it *isn't* a spelling mistake. I had this argument with the editors, and MS-Word is plain wrong. Don't you start. Look it up.

- Resist specialisation. Training staff past a sufficient minimum is generally a waste of resources. Better to have many staff who know just enough about core systems, since staff churn and layoffs mean future staffing is entirely unpredictable. One exception is the last remaining person who understands a legacy system. On no account try to replicate this person. Training will be prohibitively expensive or unobtainable, but more importantly this person dying or retiring is probably your only hope of mounting an effective business case to replace the system, as most legacy systems are cheaper, more efficient, more stable and lower risk than any new one.

- Decision making is dangerous to the organisation and the individual. Decisions are just as likely to be wrong as right. Better to either push decisions up to somebody who is sufficiently high in the organisation to neither care nor understand, or to make a collective decision by committee that can never be pinned on an individual. Committee decision-making has the added advantage of diluting most decisions to the point where they no longer present a threat.

- Treat services as assets. The value of these assets is measured by the funding and revenues these services bring to the IT organisation. When assessing value, don't forget to include one-off cash injections to recover from emergency failures or to prevent public embarrassment, along with normal BAU[1] funding. Your most decrepit services are amongst your most valuable, as they require the greatest levels of funding just to keep them functional. Impending obsolescence greatly increases the value of a service asset: the upgrade will provide large approvals of funds while minimising external disruption by changing very little of the external service.

- The key principle is that all services must provide sufficient value to the implementing staff. Select projects that contribute to a healthy résumé and skills valuable in job seeking. This ensures optimal staff participation and overcomes most resistance. The benefits returned to staff are known as Return

---

[1] BAU = business as usual

on Investment or ROI. In order to yield the best possible ROI, it is important to measure the job market on a regular basis. This is known as defining the market space.

2.2 *Service Provider*

Determine what type of service provider your IT organisation best suits. There are three Real ITSM types:

2.2.1 Type I: Internal

The IT department is internal to the customer organisation. This can be too close for comfort: there will be much transparency due to team work and the "water-cooler effect" – information obtained informally in casual conversation. This is no different to the wartime problem of "loose lips sink ships".

On the other hand, the relationship is usually defined in suitably vague terms to facilitate excuses and re-direction of blame. All sorts of Inner Circles, Smokers' Networks[1] and Kitchen Cabinets[2] may be invoked to get out of trouble.

2.2.2 Type II: Detached

IT services are provided by a separate business unit. If this model is desired, it can be created without the effort of a separate unit simply by introducing ITSM, and in particular SLAs, to provide formalised detachment.

Executives are inclined to be glad to be rid of IT so you may have to settle for a more official arrangement of a separate business unit. Formalising the terms of service introduces all sorts of distortions

---

[1] If you are not aware of the political advantage that smokers have in a Western organisation it is time you found out. The higher the rank, the more likely they are to be a smoker. So unprecedented access is had by those who huddle in doorways and car-parks sharing a cigarette break with the powerful.
[2] This has nothing to do with household furnishings. Look it up.

based on the over-simplification inherent in a document that everyone seeks to "keep simple". Ambiguities and omissions open up all sorts of possibilities.

Although the relationship is formalised, the business units remain part of one happy family, so there is still scope for evasion and abdication of responsibility through alternate informal channels.

2.2.3   Type III: Remote

The service provider is a separate organisation under contract.

This may seem the ideal model with a formal contract ensuring all sorts of distortions of deliverables, and making change almost impossible, but there is a downside. Very little is forgiven of an external organisation and much unjust blame can be put on it. It is hard enough avoiding just blame without having to deal with unwarranted blame as well.   You are now present at very few meetings.

On the other hand if Service volatility is an issue, there is no more effective mechanism for setting the existing Service Catalogue in stone than to outsource it. See *Outsourcing*, page 45.

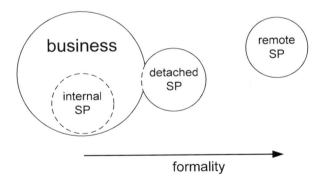

Figure 2-2   Real ITSM service providers

2.3 *Service Porthole*

It is essential to define a suitably narrow criterion for permissible services.

The Service Diameter (SD) defines the number of degrees of freedom allowed to customers when requesting services. Real ITSM is about minimising this number.

The resulting specification through which a service must pass in order to be accepted into production is known as the Service Porthole.

The following mechanisms are used in minimising the diameter of the Service Porthole:

* Service Valuation: this figure can readily be inflated beyond any CFO's pain threshold.

* Service Improvement Plan: used to divert resources that otherwise would be available for new services

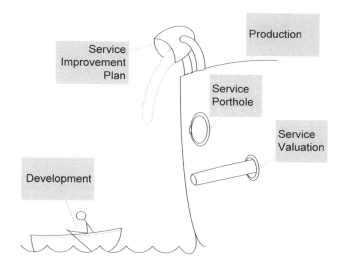

Figure 2-3 Service Porthole

2.4 Service Cataract

One of the most important documents in terms of defining the relationship between IT and its customers is the Service Cataract. This lists the available services in terms of their dependencies. The more dependencies there are for a service, the more that a customer will need to put in place first before the service is available.

The optimum position is where a service is dependant on another service or resource being in place first, which in turn has its own requirements and so on through a series of cascading dependencies that pour over the user, hence the term Service Cataract. If properly designed, the Service Cataract can ensure a service is never actually turned on. If the contract is well designed, this will not prevent IT from charging for it anyway.

Figure 2-4   Service Cataract

There are two kinds of Service Cataract:

- The Brochure Cataract, also known as the Bullshido[1] Cataract, in which we promise customers various services and service levels. Colour, multiple fonts, nice cover.

- The Technical Cataract, otherwise known as the Weasel Cataract, in which we document for internal purposes the Real ITSM Services. Black and white, small font, no cover.

---

[1] From Clive James on TV once: "the ancient Japanese art of Bullshido"

Naturally the service descriptions in these documents bear little resemblance to each other, but nobody is likely to notice so long as the services have the same name in each.

2.5 *Valuing a service*

In the design stages, value of a service is predicted on two parameters: Futility and Variability.

2.5.1 Futility

The more futile a user requirement is, the more resources can be expended and the more staff occupied without any likelihood of the service actually having to be delivered. So long as nobody is foolish enough to point out this Futility in the early stages of a service's deathcycle, the ultimate failure of the implementation can be blamed squarely on unrealistic user expectations. The business may suspect but they will never be able to pin anything.

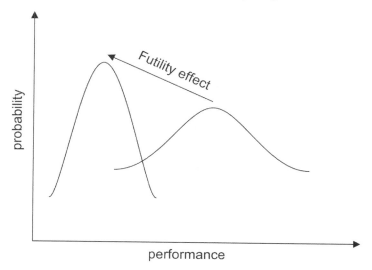

Figure 2-5   **Futility decreases the performance**

2.5.2   Variability

The higher the Variability of the possible deliverables based on the user requirements the more freedom IT has to deliver what suits instead of what is required, or alternatively to take the service development into an ultimately futile direction (see *Futility*, previous page).

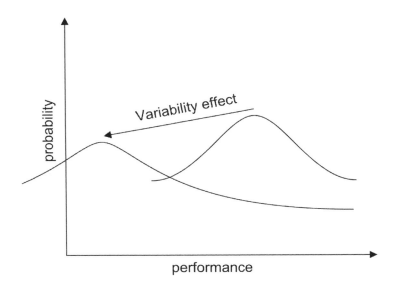

Figure 2-6   Variability reduces the performance

Assess your organisation against *Service Reaction* key practices. Score 3 for each compliance and 1 for each Bonus. Heck, score anything you like: it is **your** assessment.

Practice	score
Limit all Real financial planning to a MPFP of one year or less	
Bonus: Use MS-Excel	
Under-utilise all key resources - maintain emergency capacity	
Prohibit all optimisation, efficiency or consolidation activities	
Document only a very few procedures and enforce none of them	
Bonus: Use MS-Excel	
All reports and metrics provide only enough information to support the allocation of blame, and contain sufficient time-lag to prevent runaway feedback loops	
Bonus: Use MS-Excel	
Staff know just enough about core systems	
No replication of last remaining person who understands a legacy system	
Stamp out grass-roots initiatives	
Create initiatives only in response to an executive directive and invest the minimum necessary to prevent punishment	
Prohibit continual improvement	
Either push decisions up to somebody who is sufficiently high in the organisation to neither care nor understand, or make a collective decision by committee	
Treat services as assets and value them by the funding and revenues these services bring to the IT organisation	
Bonus: Use MS-Excel	
All services provide sufficient value to the implementing staff	
Define a suitably narrow criterion for permissible services	
Have a Service Cataract that lists the available services in terms of their dependencies	
Bonus: Use MS-Excel	
Maximise futility and variability of services	
Total	

3
Service Demand

Despite the best efforts of a Real ITSM department, customers will still want services. Peer pressure on the CIO from other departmental heads and expectations from superiors mean that some services must be delivered in order to continue funding for another year.

3.1 Designing a Service

A Real IT department will understand that, despite our best efforts, sometimes a new service is unavoidable, usually for political reasons. In this situation, three strategies are followed (the "Three Ds").

3.1.1 Design for failure

Where possible, design for failure to ensure the service never sees the light of day. There is a multitude of possible tactics. These are some examples:

- Confuse the users so as to develop ambiguous requirements that may be interpreted as IT sees fit (and the user ultimately blamed)

- Tempt the users with impossibly expensive options

- Lead the users into politically unacceptable options

- Ensure the users includes two strong power groups then get each to adopt mutually incompatible design decisions

- Allow users to change requirements at any stage.

- Expand the scope as much as possible so that the project either collapses under its own weight or takes so long the service is irrelevant by the time it is delivered

- Omit as many essential design decisions as possible

- Select a technical architecture incompatible with all incumbent technologies

- Select technologies that are unproven, still in development or - best of all - purely speculative. Vendors can provide these in abundance.

3.1.2 Delay

The IT industry has developed a wide variety of techniques for delaying a new service, so many that it is beyond the scope of this book to survey them all. Common examples include:

- Workshops, stakeholder consultation, community impact reports. See *Demand Management*, page 80.

- Expand scope (see *Design for Failure*, page 38)

- Employ external consultants (recall they are almost always paid by the hour – they are on your side on this one)

- Divert resources to "higher priorities"

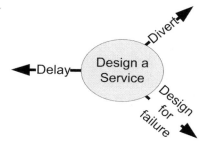

Figure 3-1 the Three Ds

3.1.3 Divert

No project ends up as originally designed. With care, the result can be entirely different and much closer to the requirements of the IT department.

- Have architects, Operations or outsourced service providers over-rule design decisions and mandate alternatives desired by IT or optimal for job seeking.

- Throughout the development of the service, whittle away parts of the service as excessively expensive or not achievable within required timeframes, especially on the run up to deadlines (see *Delay*, above)

- Substitute other design or implementation options as "functionally equivalent"

In designing a service, it is vital to take into account Total Cost of Ownership, or TCO. This must of course be maximised to ensure adequate return to the IT department.

3.2 Service Level Arguments

The Service Level Argument (SLA) documents the service targets to be aimed for by the IT department. Equally, the SLA defines the service level the business must accept. Gaining business agreement is always nice if this can be achieved. Otherwise the SLA can be unilateral.

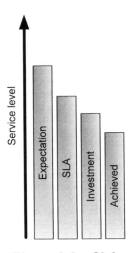

Figure 3-2   SLAs

By having a formal contractual definition, this ensures that IT and the business remain distinct, divided by the SLA. Excessive familiarity between the two groups might lead to teamwork, not in the best interests of the IT department. The SLA ensures the relationship remains adversarial.

If the SLA clearly defines a service target such as 95% availability, then IT can set spending levels so this figure is seldom if ever exceeded, thus optimising allocation of resources. Most organisations are so resource constrained that it can be successfully argued that there should be no penalties for falling short of the target. The IT department is of course doing the best it can, given the constraints under which it operates, along with those it sets itself.

Typically, organisations have limited infrastructure with which to measure service levels, and customers almost never have any. Therefore measured levels are usually estimates. When estimating levels, it is best to err on the optimistic side, in order to maintain staff morale and reduce distress for users.

It is standard practice to argue over SLAs on a regular basis with customers.

3.3 *Availability*

Design for the lowest availability level that will be tolerated by the customer.

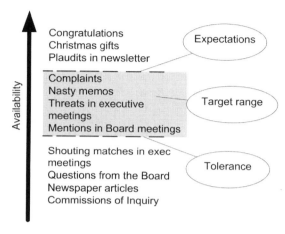

If the SLA is well designed there will be no obligation to meet it anyway, but it is important to set expectations as low as possible in order to minimise the need for User Management later.

Figure 3-3 Availability levels

24x7 services are to be preferred over more limited hours. 24x7 design means that overtime hours and allowances are designed in to the operational budget, while scheduled outage windows can more credibly be scheduled for say Tuesday lunchtime. Infrastructure must be more robust, meaning better technologies on the resume, longer implementation times, more support, and happier vendors leading to more conference invitations.

Closely related to availability is capacity. Capacity ceilings are usually blown by some unforeseeable random event anyway, so capacity planning and monitoring are pointless. In addition, blowing capacity-limits precipitates a crisis, which makes obtaining funding for new infrastructure simpler and quicker.

See also *Crisis Manager*, page 93.

3.4 *Discontinuity*

IT Discontinuity looks at maintaining systems through catastrophe. Catastrophic events are an essential part of IT management: only after a catastrophe can we obtain sufficient attention and funding from the business to ensure a robust infrastructure.

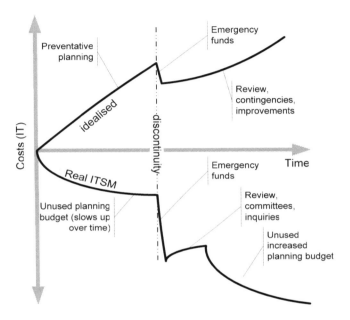

Figure 3-4   IT Discontinuity

If a discontinuity is sufficiently catastrophic, even the most basic of recoveries will attract user gratitude, and IT is seen to make great strides towards eventually restoring close to where a service was before the discontinuity.

Most discontinuities are self-generating and an adequate strategy is to wait for their arrival. This does not preclude designing a service to ensure a suitable discontinuity within a reasonable timeframe.

Discontinuities are unpredictable by nature so planning or practicing for them is pointless unless pressure from auditors becomes intolerable.

3.5   *Imposition Security*

Security systems exist only to make honest people's jobs harder.

They put an enormous support burden on IT, and they obstruct staff attempting to rectify problems or satisfy their own curiosity.

Security activity should be auditor-driven.   Minimise security infrastructure investment except under threat of losing compliance or failing audit, or even waiting until after this happens. This is called Threat Management.

Security violations do impact IT reputation and really successful ones may negatively impact next year's budgets, so the occasional forensic audit is useful. We need to prevent any loss of budget so these are known as preventative security measures. It is better if these are conducted from within IT, otherwise accidental collateral discoveries can outweigh the benefit of the audit.

3.6   *Vendor Management*

Vendors generally manage IT departments well, and little intervention is required from IT.

The greatest difficulties arise when staff squabble over who is to be a vendor's contact, since the role appeals to those who like desktop toys, or quality golf shirts or wind-cheaters, and those who like to travel. Often a rotating roster can be established, or if this proves too cumbersome then senior management should simply usurp the roles.

In order to optimise being managed by vendors, it is worth seeking to be a reference site. Being a reference site will bring benefits:

Love and attention. This requires far more vendor resource than could ever be sustained in more than a few clients, so be one of them.

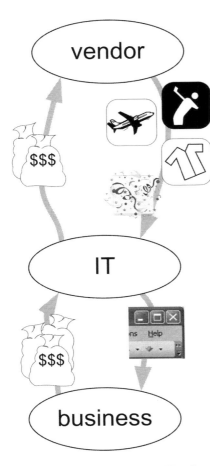

Figure 3-5   The Real IT value chain

Glory. Vendors will make you look a hero, in glossy brochures, advertisements, articles and best of all conference presentations. They will put your CIO's face on full page ads in magazines where their peers will see and then give them a poster-size framed version of the ad for their office wall.

Conferences. Research on the number of reference sites whose CIO went to the vendor's world conference at the vendor's expense as a speaker or regularly appeared on speaking tours to warm sunny countries would yield interesting results.

This works particularly well with a CIO about two years from retirement: apply love and glory, and then once they retire employ them on contract to be an overseas superstar keynote speaker at conferences in exotic places.

Celebration. In the face of defeat, declare victory. This was an old British military tactic when faced with unshakeable guerrilla insurgence: walk away and hold a victory parade. No need to admit the half-million-dollar project is a failure when you can bluff your way out of it with vocal assistance from the vendor. Tell everyone how successful it was for long enough and even your own staff might start to believe it, especially if they start getting invited to conferences in exotic places.

3.7   *Outsourcing*

Outsourcing is often perceived negatively within IT but is it in fact a beneficial and valuable phenomenon to be encouraged in the appropriate situations.

The benefits of outsourcing include:

- Efficiency: outsourcing allows staff to move to a new and larger organisation without the need for job-hunting

- Flexibility: staff moving to an outsourcer organisation have a wide range of environments and technologies to choose from

- Stability: for staff remaining within the IT organisation, outsourcing provides a stabilising influence.   Changes become high cost, slow and difficult

- Training: outsource providers have to demonstrate higher levels of certification than their customers so staff can usually advance the training part of their resumes far faster than at their previous employer

- Redundancy: staff who are so ineffective that they are not taken on by the outsourcer at least have the compensation of a redundancy payout and a better story on their résumé than having been fired

- Retirement: where staff are approaching retirement age, outsourcing and the consequent redundancy should of course be embraced as a way to maximise retirement savings

- Accountability: above all other benefits, outsourcing provides an extremely effective transfer of accountability out of the IT organisation

Assess your organisation against *Service Demand* key practices. Score 3 for each compliance and 1 for each Bonus.

Practice	score
Total from page 35	
Design for failure	
Delay new services	
Divert new services to better fit IT requirements	
Have formal SLAs and argue over SLAs on a regular basis with customers	
Bonus: Use MS-Excel	
Design for the lowest availability level that will be tolerated by the customer	
Treat capacity planning and monitoring as pointless	
Wait for service discontinuities and/or design services to ensure a suitable discontinuity within a reasonable timeframe	
Do not plan or rehearse for service discontinuities unless pressure from auditors becomes intolerable	
Minimise security infrastructure investment except under threat of losing compliance or failing audit	
Bonus: Wait until *after* this happens	
Perform occasional forensic audits from within IT	
Have a system to allocate vendor contacts	
Bonus: Rotate contacts to share the value	
Seek to be a reference site for all purchases	
Encourage outsourcing in the appropriate situations	
Total	

4
Service Taming

In the unlikely event that a service makes it to production implementation, it is the IT department's responsibility to ensure that it is implemented with minimum impact on the existing IT environment.

This involves

- delaying implementation

- fitting the service to the existing platforms and processes

- setting user expectations low so that they can readily be met

- minimising the cost and impact of testing and deployment.

Any sort of control at all is a bonus.

4.1   Capture, Tag and Release

The primary function of Service Taming is Capture, Tag and Release (also known as "the three Ds": Detect, Designate and Disperse).

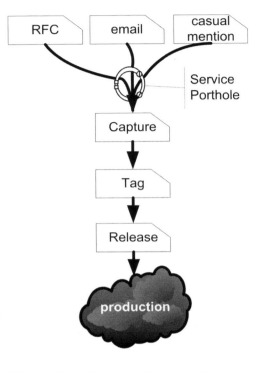

The first that IT Operations will hear about a new service is normally the Change Control request for it to go into production, i.e. its face pops up at the Service Porthole.   At times this is the first the entire IT department knows about it, but invariably it is news to Operations.   This is known as Capture.   It provides Operations with an opportunity to examine the new service for the first time.

Figure 4-1   Capture Tag and Release

The Operations staff needs to be ready with strong pre-prepared excuses to reject it.   This is known as Operational Readiness.

Sadly, most services have an unstoppable momentum by this stage, and it is all Operations can do to provide their own name for the service (this is known as Tag) and then abdicate all control over it (Release).

A service is Tagged using terminology understood by and relevant to only the IT department, such as the network identifier of the server on which it runs.

The purpose of Tagging a service is to ensure security and confidentiality of IT Operations communications. IT Operations staff should be trained in the art of forgetting all other names for the service.

Because the service has been designed without monitoring tools or metrics, the IT Operations group then Release it into production, into the wild, where it exists and evolves mostly without their input or awareness.

> *If you love something set it free. If it comes back it is yours. If it doesn't then it never was.*

This reduces system overheads and frees up Operations staff for reconfiguring infrastructure devices, testing new technologies, and acting as vendor references.

4.2 *Change*

Don't.

Where you have no choice but to break this rule, rigorous Change Control is essential to provide an adequate brake on the processing.

This is one area where meticulous record-keeping is a benefit, as is inclusive review by all stakeholders and careful deliberate decision-making reviewed at all levels.

See also *Crisis Manager*, page 93.

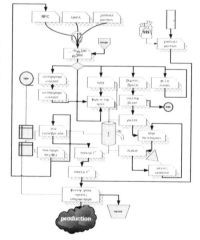

Figure 4-2 Real simple change process

4.3 *Stuff*

Known elsewhere as "assets" or "configuration", Real ITSM manages Stuff. Records should be kept of all Stuff except where records are not kept.

The key Stuff activities are:

4.3.1 Collation

Management or auditors will periodically demand lists of Stuff. Given that their requirements are entirely random and unpredictable, the most efficient way to deal with this is to respond on an ad-hoc basis by reallocating staff to collate the data.

This is known as on-demand processing. The technology of choice is MS-Excel.

4.3.2 Implication

The Byzantine complexity of the modern IT environment means that the only device capable of grasping the implications of a change or failure in one component is wetware. Vendors claim that software tools exist with this miraculous ability but only a human can understand whether it matters that one server is out in a load-balanced farm of web servers supporting UDDI lookup to Web Services providing functionality common across four applications. You need a CMDB called Sue. Make sure more than one person can do this, and keep them happy.

Even if you implement the most advanced artificial intelligence available to deduce the conceptual structures in the data, sooner or later it is going to do something really dumb. Just once. And from then on everyone will go ask the wetware expert anyway, to double-check what it says.

4.3.3 CMDB building.

We don't need one, but we have to have one. Everyone else is. The books say so. It would be neat. This is the area of Real ITSM worst affected by Excessive Technical Fastidiousness, or ETF (discussed further in *Categorisation*).

The best strategy is to decide to build a bespoke custom CMDB. The resulting project will happily run for years designing, data modelling, coding, integrating, extracting and reporting, best known as "the three D's": Design, Development, and Data.

Figure 4-3   Vendor CMDB

Second best strategy is to buy one. Nobody can actually sell you one of course. CMDB is an aspirational concept, like holiness, or honesty.

The tools foisted on us by the vendors are asset databases with bells on, or network monitors with a whistle on top, or desktop managers with fluffy dice. This means you will embark on a customisation and integration project that is close to the effort required for the roll-your-own CMDB.

And then there is the data population exercise. If you have made the data model sufficiently broad and fine-grained (which is where they all end up) then you can keep several staff amused for years just finding, loading, labelling and inter-relating all the Stuff.

Either way, go for the full solution from the start: phased approaches might actually finish.

4.4 Knowledge

The central foundation of all Real ITSM spending and staff utilisation is the Bottomless Knowledge Management System, or BKMS. This system stores not only the IT objects that IT happens to have a record of, but also:

- Parking lot utilisation statistics

- User health records and personal files (useful for troublesome users)

- Real-time sports results (for obvious reasons)

- Growth rates and mortality of office plants

- Transactional data from decommissioned systems, just in case

- Cubicle dimensional data

- Supplier satisfaction surveys

- The Guinness Book of Records

…and in fact all data that can be found regardless of its relevance to services.

All data is tagged with a manually-assigned 17 character identifier, inter-related in an n-way web of relationships (with customised graphical explorer software).

The lowest cost BKMS employs a WMRN[1] storage structure.

Such a project will ensure ever increasing funding, maximum staff utilisation, and very happy suppliers.

---

[1] **Write Many Read Never, as compared to say Write Once Read Many. The simplest instance of WMRN is an unconnected wire.**

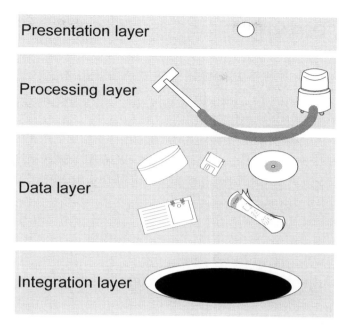

Presentation layer

Processing layer

Data layer

Integration layer

Figure 4-4   BKMS

4.5 *Culture*

Apparently a major source of failure of service implementations is failure to understand the culture of the IT staff.

IT culture is an amalgam of sports results, current television shows, conspiracy theories, malicious gossip, reminiscence about old technology, lust over new technology, celebrity mating, holiday plans and the bodily functions of babies. It is absurdly easy to understand, so Real ITSM does not recognise this as an issue.

4.6 Testing

It is rumoured that in some organisations testing is performed by groups other than the developers themselves, but insufficient evidence exists to confirm this so it is not yet considered Real ITSM.

Testing is best left to those who developed it, as they understand it best. Professional testers seem to find many extra test cases that only prolong implementation cycles. It is much more efficient to do all testing in the development team.

Assess your organisation against *Service Taming* key practices. Score 3 for each compliance and 1 for each Bonus.

Practice	score
Total from page 46	
Capture all services going into production	
Bonus: Use MS-Excel	
Operations staff have strong pre-prepared excuses to reject new services	
Tag services using terminology understood by and relevant to only the IT department	
Bonus: Use network IDs or invoice numbers	
Release new services into production, without input or awareness	
Minimise and retard change	
Bonus: Don't change	
Records kept of all Stuff except where records are not kept	
Bonus: Use MS-Access	
Respond to demands for lists of Stuff on demand	
Bonus: Use MS-Excel	
Have a wetware CMDB	
Bonus: ... called Sue	
Have a project building or implementing a software CMDB	
Bonus: No phased approach	
Have a Bottomless Knowledge Management System	
Bonus: Use WMRN storage	
Ignore culture	
Do all testing in the development team	
Total	

5
Service Nursing

By the time a service is in production, the rigours of design, development and deployment will mean that it is almost certainly unstable, unsuited and unmanageable.

Accepting that a service has - despite best endeavours - found its way into production, IT should make the best of it by nursing the service along to an extended lifetime with a minimum of investment, thereby maximising the return to the department.

The functions of Service Nursing are

- minimising the impact on the department

- redirecting or obscuring accountability

- mitigating the reputational damage

- reducing the activity from users to tolerable levels.

5.1 Problems

Why it is that problems are one of the most neglected areas of ITSM is a mystery. We have the place to track them in any Service Desk tool worth the licence fee.

Fixing problems gives geeks something to do besides meddling with system settings or moving stuff. It makes users happy. IT wants services to last as long as possible. It is a win-win.

Real ITSM considers problems to be the most important area of Service Nursing.

Problems are much too important to slap Problem Management on them. Once there is a process with an owner and procedures and meetings and problem records, everyone can relax and go back to neglecting them. Just fix them.

Problems suffer from the important/urgent dilemma (see Figure 5-1). They are very important but seldom urgent enough to get attention over the incoming bombardment of incidents.

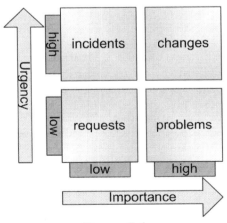

Figure 5-1

5.2   *Telephone*

The Real ITSM monitoring device is the Telephone.   This device is extremely sensitive to any interruption to service and will ring within a time inversely proportional to the importance of the service to users.

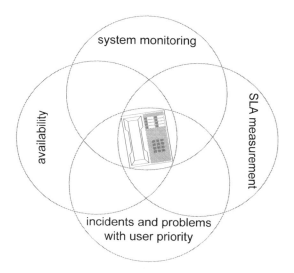

Figure 5-2   Telephone system

Not only that, but it will tell the Service Desk precisely what the impact is, and the required restoration time.

Therefore the Telephone renders redundant all the complex systems management tools, event monitors, alerts, service catalogues and other encumbrances employed by other ITSM frameworks.

It is cheap to implement, uses redundant systems, has very high availability, requires little administration, and its implementation and maintenance are outsourced.

It is an exemplary piece of state-of-the-art IT equipment.

5.3 Service Desk

The Service Desk is an essential component of Service Nursing. It can be considered as an ancillary support function of the Telephone.

As well as essential monitoring and tuning information, the Telephone system unfortunately also suffers from high levels of "noise".

It is the Service Desk's function to filter out this noise (such as complaints, feedback, and appeals for help) from the useful availability data and the occasional problem.

The Service Desk can also be seen as a buffer for the IT department from the rest of the organisation (see *User Management*, page 77).

The Service Desk is made up of three components:

5.3.1 People

Try to get people who actually like other human beings. An IQ in triple digits is useful.

The travel industry is a good place to recruit: they are friendly and polite, they can work with urgency, they understand closure, and anyone who can work Galileo and Magellan booking systems has enough IT nous.

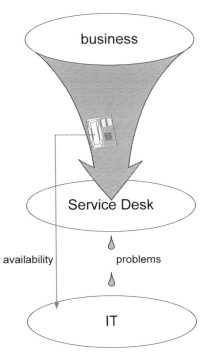

Figure 5-3 Real Service Desk

5.3.2   Software

The only place ITIL specifies the functionality of software is the one place where it is complete rubbish, i.e. CMDB.   Real ITSM understands that the one place where software matters is Service Desk.

If you can store people, contacts, requests, incidents, problems, changes, and assets in one place with transferable ownership (i.e. horizontal/functional escalation), and you can store and manage downloaded digital music, you are there – you have all the essential software to do Real ITSM.   Everything else can be done in Excel or by Telephone.

5.3.3   Rules, procedures, notifications

These fall on the Service Desk staff like rain.

It is worth noting at this point that email is not communication.   Nor are any of the digital buckets such as folders, portals, document management systems, knowledge-bases, or wikis.   Proper communication is not a one-way push.

There is a two-phase confirmation in Real Communication.   This is most effectively done with an unfashionable technique known as "talking".

Regular staff meetings with group discussion and informational briefings are essential if the Service Desk is to hold off the business successfully.

5.4 Requests

Real ITSM considers all requests from users to be a Request[1]. After sufficient information is obtained, Real Requests can be classified as[2]:

- Incident: An Incident is defined by Real ITSM as an unplanned interruption to the normal operation of IT or a reduction in the quality of the perception of IT.

  A Major Incident is one with a significant risk of the Board of Directors (or Minister/Secretary) hearing about it, or of it getting into the newspapers. See *Damage Management*, page 82.

- Request For Change: Some organisations allow users to open RFCs directly, others have some form of gating process such as Requests. Real ITSM requires gating via a Request, as one more step in delaying change.

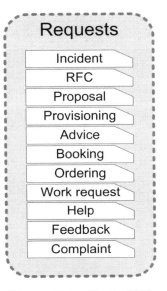

Figure 5-4 Real ITSM requests

- Proposals: The Service Desk can be a front-end to the demand component of project portfolio management. Think of it as a request for project. These should be declined or ignored for as long as user patience lasts: see *Demand Management*, page 80.

- Provisioning: User requires access to a service or part of a service, e.g. security permission, menu option, digital certificate,

---

[1] This would seem logical but ITIL still hasn't done this as of version 3
[2] This list originally appeared in the author's article *The Evolution of the ITIL Request* on www.ITSMWatch.com
http://www.itsmwatch.com/itil/article.php/3705936

client install, desktop device, phone, etc. These are also best ignored (see *Access*, page 69).

- Advice: How do I …? Should I …? Which is the best way to …? This category needs to be closely linked to the Known Idiot database, see page 79. And ignored.

- Booking: Scheduled attendance at training, seminar, meeting, reservation of a resource, annual leave. Also best ignored, especially if users have an alternate path for doing this themselves.

- Ordering: Books, desks, catering, stationery, travel... See *Booking*, above.

- Work Request: Run a report. Move a PC. Install a projector. Paint the kitchen. These make good busywork that draws resources away from projects that are moving too quickly.

- Help: Correcting data arising from user error, restoring a deleted file, sending a document, untangling a mess. Likewise good busywork.

- Feedback: praise, suggestion, idea. Praise should be immediately forwarded to management, while other feedback is best omitted from reporting in the interests of brevity.

- Complaint: complaints are a form of feedback but they are best dealt with separately, so that they can be ignored in a more focused manner and so they can be reported separately (or not at all).

5.5   *Incident priority*

Some organisations give high importance to how long IT is going to take to resolve incidents, and they write this into SLAs as a key metric.   Usually high priority incidents are to be resolved quickly while lower priority incidents can take progressively longer.

This is akin to firemen promising to extinguish three-alarm fires within ten minutes but a backyard grassfire may take until tomorrow. It is absurd on three levels: extinguishing the fire takes as long as it takes, bigger fires take longer, and that little yard fire won't be so small tomorrow.

While we are on the topic of firemen, it should be noted that firemen spend an awful lot of time polishing the fire engine, rolling and unrolling hoses, and playing cards.   Any manager who expects Service Desk and Level One Support people to be always busy ("fully utilised") does not understand what they do.   Real Level One Support has plenty of spare capacity.

Real ITSM SLAs don't define response times.   Based on priority, they define how many people will be assigned to an incident; how many hours a day it will be worked on; and what gets overruled to work on it. See Table 5-1   Real ITSM Priorities.

Because Real Priority (also known as Care Factor) is measured by the number of metaphorical fans that are being hit by effluent, it starts at zero and goes up.

This is much more logical than other systems where 1 is highest. Just when you thought you had seen the worst thing that can go wrong, something comes along that makes all past priority 1 incidents look mild. How can you communicate this? With Real ITSM, you simply assign it a priority that is one higher than any previous incident.

Priority	Number of Staff Assigned	Hours per day	Person managing response	We will pull staff from
0	1	.0025	Peon	Reading the newspaper
1	1	4	Geek	Web surfing
2	2	8	Service Desk Team Leader	Staff meetings
3	4	8	Service Delivery Manager	Training courses
4	8	24	Operations Manager	Projects
5	16	100	CIO	Home
6	Everyone	1000	CEO	Leave
7	Including ex-employees	∞	Bill Gates	Honeymoon

Table 5-1   Real ITSM Priorities

Many calls are priority zero. The drek isn't flying. Because users seem to have an aversion to being told this, Real ITSM tracks Real Priority (what IT thinks it is) and User Priority (what the user thinks it is). These often have an inverse relationship.

"Yes sir, we understand that you see this as a Priority 7 and we are [substitute fabrication here]"

In the same way that Real Priority is conceptually measured in number of fans, the User Priority can be thought of as being measured in the number of dummies being spat.

The activity of dealing with incoming incidents is covered in User Management.

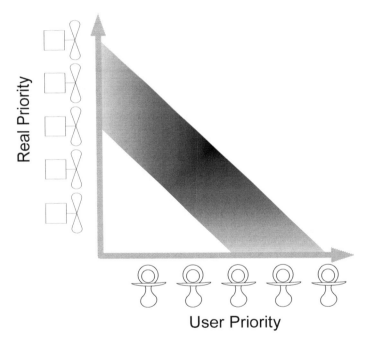

Figure 5-5   Real vs. User Priority

5.6 *Escalation*

A phone list is always useful, but Real ITSM hierarchic escalation depends on wetware again: customer relationship managers. Any list, document, database or – heaven forbid – CMDB will not provide useful escalation contact data.   Either the names or numbers will be out of date; politics will dictate a different escalation path; or the persons concerned will be uncontactable.

We have spent three hundred thousand years evolving techniques to communicate with each other. Digital technology has a long way to go to replace this. Ask someone.

5.7 *Categorisation*

Another area that agitates the perfectionists among us is categorisation; of services, incidents, problems, changes, assets, pencils…

Categorisation of requests is one of the most common areas to be affected by Excessive Technical Fastidiousness or ETF (the worst affected area is CMDB). Many technical people like completeness and accuracy, not to mention a fondness for neat, clever, intricate solutions whether there is a problem or not. The result is ETF: an obsession with doing it **right**, whether or not this is a useful use of time, yields a good return on investment, or is the most sensible use of available funds – i.e. whether or not it makes business sense.

Every taxonomy degenerates into either unusable complexity or banal simplicity. A heroic effort can clean up categorisation, re-categorise everything properly and – very occasionally – properly train staff on how to use it, but this level of effort must be sustained in order for the taxonomy to remain useful. There is never a good business case for this level of investment in ongoing ownership, so we end up after a while with 95% categorised as Miscellaneous, Other, General, Admin or Unknown.

It is far more efficient and less soul-destroying to perform on-demand processing (see also *Collation of Stuff,* page 50). When statistics are required to support decision-making then take a good sized random sample, manually categorise to whatever taxonomy is currently preferred, and fire up Excel.

N.B. Real managers don't need statistics to make decisions anyway. Real managers use statistics to confirm gut instincts and the opinions of their staff.

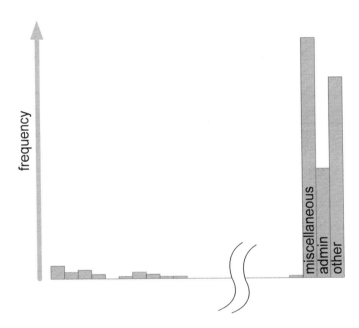

Figure 5-6   Category frequency

5.8 Applications

IT Operations should not try to tell Development how to do their jobs – they will just see you off. Operations may be able to influence the early stages of application design. The way to do this is via the Architects who occasionally have some influence and who love to add yet more layers and boxes to their models. Another way is to go directly to projects and beg.

Real ITSM ignores all development projects for as long as possible (usually until the RFC for production rollout), then tries to enforce Operational Acceptance Criteria for as long as possible on the incoming system before being steamrolled by executive management and then implementing it "ready or not". The benefits of this approach are minimal effort through the lifecycle of the application development, maximum project resources through and beyond go live, and abdication of responsibility for the production system.

5.9 Access

Giving users access to systems is usually the most annoying activity that IT is obliged to perform. In extreme cases IT is even expected to take access away again. There are two Real ITSM ways to deal with this problem. Choose depending on whether staff are currently under-utilised or over-utilised.

1) design and implement complex automated processes to grant and approve access then empower users to do it themselves

2) take so long to provision that users give up and share logins

Assess your organisation against *Service Nursing* key practices. Score 3 for each compliance and 1 for each Bonus.

Total from page 55	
Track problems and fix them	
Bonus: Use Post-It Notes®	
Monitor and measure service using Telephone	
Detect incidents and problems using Telephone	
Determine impact and priority using Telephone	
Service Desk filters out noise and passes availability data and the occasional problem.	
Use Service Desk software	
Talk to Service Desk staff	
All requests from users are a Request, later classified	
Major Incidents trigger Damage Management	
RFCs require a request first	
Bonus: Must ask nicely	
Project proposals require a request	
Most requests are ignored	
Bonus: ... forever	
Complaints are carefully ignored	
Bonus: Not reported	
Level One Support has plenty of spare capacity	
Priority starts at zero and goes up	
Track Real Priority and User Priority	
Track hierarchic escalation using wetware	
Categorise Stuff on demand	
Bonus: Use MS-Excel	
Ignore projects for as long as possible, then try to enforce Operational Acceptance Criteria	
Either automate or ignore user access provisioning	
Total	

6

Continual Service Assessment

Given that the IT department's first priority is stability, production services should remain unchanged as much as possible. So the ongoing focus is on continual service assessment in order to show that the service is adequate; that IT is delivering to approximately the desired service level; and that other services are of a higher priority for attention.

Real ITSM Continual Service Assessment (CSA) provides opportunities for considerable resource investment in service level measurement, which employs staff, keeps executive management happy and diverts customers.

It also creates opportunity for indefinitely ongoing maturity assessment, which keeps consultants economically viable. It is most important to keep Parasites (often referred to as "partners") solvent. They hold significant amounts of the IT organisation's intellectual property. They also provide otherwise unobtainable access to executive management, and a layer of valuable credibility.

6.1 CSA model

CSA follows a continually repeated 3-Step Assessment Activity[1]:

1) Measure something

2) Analyse the data to show that the service is adequate and IT is delivering to approximately the desired service level

3) File the report

There is an alternate CSA model that follows an amended cycle:

1) Measure something

2) Analyse the data

3) Destroy the report

Originating in Florida, USA, this variant is commonly referred to as Miami CSA.

---

[1] This Activity doesn't actually do anything interesting and it does not relate to any other accepted model so the best name we could come up with is "3-Step". There are other processes around that have the same problem.

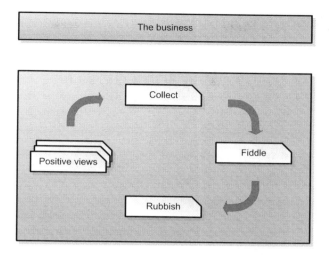

Figure 6-1   **Service reporting process**

6.1.1   Service Level Management

Arguably, Service Level Management should be integral to CSA, but the Real SLM authors don't talk to the Real CSA authors so we will just mention it incidentally here and invent the separate CSA model shown above that bears no relation to anything else generally accepted in the industry.

6.2 Gap analysis

Gap analysis identifies the difference between the current state and where IT would ideally like to be in terms of activity maturity.

The *Maturity Model* section, page 16, specifies the optimum maturity as 1, with 0 as an acceptable alternative. Unlike other less helpful frameworks, Real ITSM provides defined maturity assessment criteria. Go to www.realitsm.com to download an assessment spreadsheet of Real Practice. Using these criteria, assess current maturity and plot on a "radar chart" such as the example shown here. The most important gaps can be readily identified.

Perform this assessment regularly. Only act on it if there is an urgent need to occupy some staff resources.

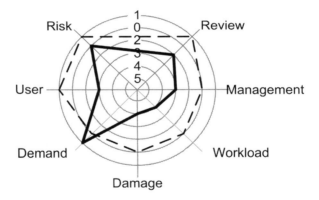

Figure 6-2 Real ITSM maturity chart

Assess your organisation against *Continual Service Assessment* key practices. Score 3 for each compliance and 1 for each Bonus.

Practice	score
Total from page 70	
Follow 3-Step Assessment Activity or Miami CSA	
Regularly assess compliance and perform gap analysis	
Total	

7
Real ITSM Activities

Assessment of Real ITSM organisations can return maturity of zero for some of the ITIL processes (no detectable process) and One for many of them (process is anarchic). This might lead the assessor to wonder if anyone is doing anything, but this would be unfair. There are high levels of activity in real IT shops: it is simply that the ITIL model fails to recognise them.

So for the benefit of ITSM assessors everywhere, here are the Real ITSM activities that make up Real Practice.

7.1 Risk Management

Specific risk areas are covered in other activities, such as User Management, Management Management, Progress Management and Review Management, but Real ITSM requires a central function to track these risks across the entire IT department, and to ensure that steps are under way to mitigate them.

Since managers themselves are often one of the higher risks to the department, the Real Risk Register should be maintained somewhere where management will be unable to find it, such as on the information portal on the intranet, or under the TV magazines in the staffroom.

Risk Register			
Restricted: For approved eyes only			
Description	**Actions**	**Status**	**Scapegoat**
1 ITIL maturity assessment by Purple Antelope consulting	1/7/08 agreement to limit scope to datacentre 3/8/08 PA agree to right of review by Ops Mgr	DefCon Three	Previous CIO

Table 7-1   **Sample Real Risk Register**

7.2 *User Management*

Without proper management, users can be an unmitigated nuisance to the IT department. It falls to the ITSM functions to ensure that users do not have a negative impact on day-to-day IT operations, and within ITSM it is the Service Desk team who take the brunt.

The Service Desk performs important functions:

- monitor by telephone (see *Service Nursing*, page 57)

- buffering surges in user activity, especially using queue overflow and baulking to cap user calls

- providing the thick skin of the IT department

- call resolution through attrition

Most incoming Requests fall into one of two categories:

- PBCK: Problem Between Chair and Keyboard

- PBND: Problem Between Need and Delivery

Put another way, either the user got it wrong or someone else did.

If the Service Desk is over-servicing the user base, then some of the calls will also be simple calls for help. In a properly run Real ITSM Service Desk, users don't bother.

Software vendors learnt long ago that the vendors who over-service the customer base are the ones who go out of business, while the successful ones reduce service levels to the point where the consequent loss of customers is almost starting to outweigh the cost of improving service. This is known as Service Level Management (SLM), a concept that seems to have been totally misunderstood by the general ITSM community.

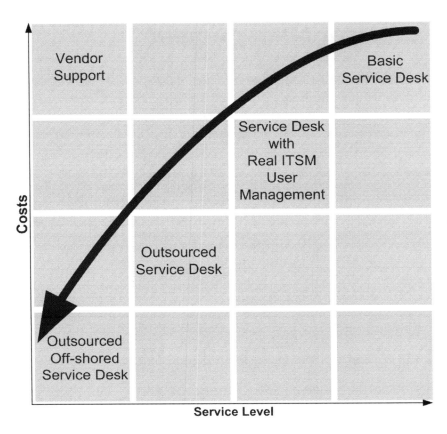

Figure 7-1   Service Level Management

Continually improving service levels is another name for continually increasing the cost of servicing the customer, which is not a good business model.

In Real ITSM, it is the role of the Service Desk to use SLM to reduce the cost and effort of service to the users until the levels of protest are intolerable or the risk of lost funding is too high.

Incoming contacts - whether they are requests, incidents, changes or insults – all fall into two categories:

1) Calls that can be resolved quickly and easily to the user's satisfaction. Resolve them.

2) Calls that are difficult or expensive to resolve. If they stem from a problem, resolve it. If not, either (a) put the call in a queue somewhere and hope to wear the user down by attrition or (b) provide the user with a resolution to something different. If they come back, repeat.

All contacts must be logged, in order to demonstrate how understaffed the Service Desk is. For this reason, it can be useful to log Requests several times, closing them each time a potential resolution is suggested or the user takes more than say an hour to call back.

On the other hand, if it is certain that the Request is finally resolved, it is best not to be too hasty in closing it until, say, the next financial year, as the number of open Requests is also a useful metric for showing how overworked the ITSM group is.

7.2.1   Known Idiot

In order to save a lot of wasted effort, Real Practice is to maintain a Known Idiot database, which can be readily searched by Service Desk operators to assist in speedy resolution of incidents.

The Known Idiot data is maintained primarily by Level One and Two Support as they resolve Incidents, but Idiots may also be identified by other staff as well.

All Known Idiots should have an associated Runaround: an effective means to divert them or keep them occupied until a final resolution can be identified (such as transfer, retirement, firing or assassination).

7.3   Demand Management

Most requests for new services are crushed by Service Demand practices, but at some point customers will become sufficiently irate that they demand new services, and take these demands to the highest levels of the organisation. It is at this point that Demand Management activities are invoked to minimise the outages and restore regular services as quickly as possible in the face of such potentially disruptive demands.

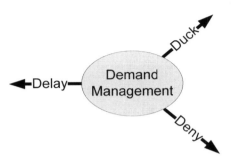

Figure 7-2   the Three Ds

Demand management activities fall into three broad categories: Delay, Deny, and Duck - the "Three Ds". See also *Designing a Service*, page 38.

7.3.1   Delay

Initially Demand Management can send customers back to better refine their initial requirement. Once this wears off, we enter a repeating cycle of consultation, workshops, prioritisation and review.

The question of prioritisation is important. Whilst Real ITSM seeks to maximise the funding for the IT department, it is essential that this be constructed in such a way as to *minimise* the funding available for new projects, or at least to minimise the *apparent* available funding.

In this way, a gating mechanism is set up that throttles project demand.

We can amplify the effect by increasing the estimated cost of preferred projects, and by giving preference to high-cost projects, especially projects favoured by executive management which fortunately tend to be very high cost anyway.

7.3.2   Deny

The alternative tactic is to kill proposals stone dead. Since most business cases are flimsily constructed speculations, it is equally easy to construct a case which shows a negative return on a project.

However this then degenerates into a political arm wrestle, and IT departments practicing Real ITSM tend not to be well placed politically.

More effective is to demonstrate that the project does not align with strategic direction, especially if it can be shown to compete with funds for an executive's pet project.

Finally Real ITSM allows a proposal to advance to initial scoping phase, where the

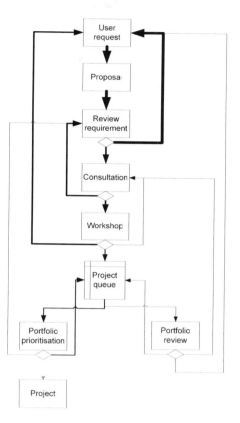

Figure 7-3 Project Demand management

scope can easily be built up to a cost-prohibitive level through requirements for continuity, reporting, audit trails, security, integration and standards compliance, amongst others.

7.3.3   Duck

The project is passed to a business unit, a vendor, consultants, anyone at all.   See *Buck Manager*, page 92.

7.4   Damage Management

Some cultures take a risk-averse approach, planning for all contingencies and minimising risks.   Other cultures are more laissez faire, preferring to economise on mitigation and take the hit on occasional consequences.   In the analogy of the grasshopper and the ant, most grasshoppers end up getting fed, whether they have to beg borrow or steal it (e.g. by becoming Seasonal Provisioning Consultants).   The required frantic burst of energy can be seen as more economical than the long grind of the ant.

Real ITSM understands that circumstances differ and a grasshopper strategy may not work in say astronautics, or explosives manufacturing.   On the other hand, technical people are often perfectionists who have trouble understanding "good enough" (they suffer from ETF) and become overly wedded to the ant strategy.

Either way, occasionally the effluent hits the air movement device, whatever our approach to risk.   The top priority then is of course to minimise damage to the IT department, which is the role of Damage Management.

To do this, Real ITSM defines a Damage Control function.   This group has the skills and tools for the "Three Ds": Divert attention, Direct blame and Defend IT.

In Major Incidents, the Damage Control team will call a meeting of the Emergency Damage Advisory Board, or EDAB, made up of the CIO, IT unit heads, and Damage Control's Public Relations Officer.

There are useful techniques available to fulfil Damage Management's objectives:

7.4.1   Divert attention

It is unfair for IT to get all the attention if users are suffering.   IT can demonstrate sensitivity to the plight of users.

* Sympathise with affected end users

- Rally efforts to help out

- Start an even bigger crisis

7.4.2   Direct blame

IT should test the resilience of relationships.

- Blame suppliers. Most vendors or service providers will take one for the team in order to protect revenue

- When called in to explain to senior executives make sure to mention unclear and changing user requirements

7.4.3   Defend IT

Loyalty is a virtue.

- Pull out any statistics that show high user satisfaction (see *BS*, page 99), or that this is a one off, or that service levels are still at or near agreed thresholds

- Point to falling budgets, staff churn, runaway projects, public holidays, high humidity…

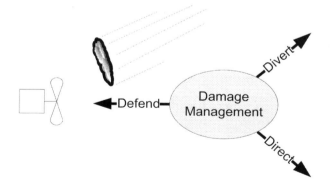

Figure 7-4   the Three Ds

7.5 Workload Management

In the last millennium, Information Technology was the cutting edge career for the nation's best and brightest. It was acceptable to work long hours and weekends; to have dinners, movies and children's sports interrupted by the pager or mobile phone; to process emails late at home. This was the price we paid for money and prestige.

As IT matures, it is discovering professionalism, certification, process and discipline. As a result it is becoming as exciting as chemical engineering and not as well paid. Now the majority of IT roles are considered advanced clerical functions. Being "in IT" does not hold the same cachet it once did. Now we say it in a bored voice, like, you know, in IT.

In order to make the future trend clear, consider this: some of the most prestigious highly trained technical careers in past centuries included typist, telephonist, steam engine driver, welder, and DBA. IT pay rates are high, but not all of them. Many have been fairly static for some time. While "leading edge" skills demand good dollars, some IT skills and roles are becoming run of the mill, and paid accordingly.

So it is no longer reasonable to expect 24-hour slavery from IT employees, but management have not noticed yet for some strange reason.

A newly emergent function in IT departments is Workload Management, whose primary activities are:

- Ensuring time and resource estimates contain sufficient allowance to permit a normal life

- Creating busywork to fill schedules

- Repelling attempts to redeploy or press-gang staff onto projects or – worse still – out of IT altogether

7.5.1   Progress Management

Progress Management is an important subset of Workload Management, where the progress of projects is closely monitored and – if necessary – slowed, to ensure minimum rate of change in the production environment, reduced pressure on project staff, and plenty of time to prepare the target infrastructure during normal work hours (9:30 – 15:30 Monday to Thursday)

IT departments should establish a Progress Management Office to centralise skills and knowledge of project retardation, to prioritise across project portfolios to identify those most in need of braking, and to provide common templates and tools for progress slowing.

One of the most effective mechanisms for slowing a project is the RFC (a.k.a. Request for Chains) which allows IT Operations a range of opportunities: requests for further information, postponed CAB meetings, requirements for further documentation or testing, and outright rejection for incorrect just-about-anything.

Another important tool is the Cant Chart, which tracks interdependencies between tasks in a graphical way, in order to show why certain tasks can't be done yet.

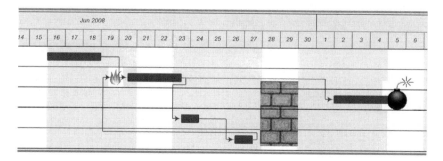

Figure 7-5   Cant Chart

7.6   *Management Management*

IT has developed a culture of unqualified people being smart enough to work out new roles thrust upon them.   This was how it had to be in the early days of the industry and the habits formed are only now beginning to fade.

As a result one common type of IT manager

- Has been promoted from a technical role, not because they are suited for management but because the organisation offers no other career path

- Lacks formal management training

- Does not like their role

As these managers develop the sociopathic nature necessary to survive the role, they become unpleasant and difficult to work with.

Another common type of manager has been brought in for their management skills but as a consequence does not understand near as much about IT as their staff do.

They have difficulty establishing rapport with geeks, and especially struggle with gaining their respect.   They struggle to differentiate between advice that is typical IT whining and that which contains valid objections to a proposal, so they are driven by the external customers, which further alienates them from their staff.

These stereotypes are common enough that IT staff have developed Management Management for their own protection.   The key deliverables of Management Management are to:

- Steer managers towards the desired decision, through the use of FUD (see *Tools* below), analyst reports, and in-house product trials and evaluations, known as Keeping Away From Sharp Objects.

- Protect staff from bad decisions, by neutralising the decision, or killing its spawned projects, called Mopping Up The Mess.

- Keep managers out of their hair, by preoccupying them with strategy and plans, statistical analysis, HR problems, or anything that happens somewhere else, known as Playing With The Car-keys.

In the extreme case, Management Management is used to drive a manager away.

Technical people have the ability to be so intractable as to make mules look supportive, safe in the knowledge that their specialist skills (and all those Perl scripts they wrote) make them difficult to replace.

They also have an uncanny ability to be totally inept at everything but a single narrow skill, at which they are the only person in the organisation who can do it. Whether this is simulated or real is cause for much debate.

In other words technical staff are well qualified to drive a manager to distraction. In the past the metric for success of these ventures was packs-a-day, but in these non-smoking times more subtle indices are required such as levels of medication or hours spent in the gym or number of facial tics.

Figure 7-6   Manager
Management

7.6.1   Tools

For Management Management, IT staff have adopted a tool originally used on them by software vendors[1]: Fear Uncertainty and Doubt, or FUD. Technical managers are FUDded over their lack of understanding of the political power games within the organisation, and non-technical managers are FUDded over technology.

Other important MM tools are:

- Management Information Systems, Executive Information Systems, data warehouses, dashboards, reports... any source of bulk data that will keep them in their office

- Evaluation spreadsheets. All evaluation spreadsheets must include weightings. The manipulation of weightings makes any result possible.

- Magazines. One of the most effective ways to get a manager to do something is to find an article in a trade magazine recommending it.

- Analyst white papers. Likewise anything written by Parasites.

- Vendors and consultants. Highly paid people in suits are viewed as a more reliable source of ideas than people who are committed to an organisation and work there all day. Make them earn their cut.

- Briefings and casual conversations. Take any one-on-one opportunity to seed an idea which – so long as the discussion is private - will usually return as the manager's idea not long afterwards. Giving up the kudos is the toll to proceed.

---

[1] Its invention is often attributed to IBM. Mind you, so is ITIL's.

7.7   *Review management*

Last but certainly not least is Review Management. An uncontrolled review has the potential to do even more damage than a rogue manager or an incident with no PR[1] spin.

Whether it is as small as a post-change review or as large as an ISO9000 audit; whether it is internal or external; every single review of the IT department's activities must be rigorously managed.

The key functions of Review Management are:

- Reviewer briefing and lunching

- Data pre-processing

- Staff coaching (in some cases it is best to relocate staff temporarily)

- Reviewer personal profiling (you never know if you will find something useful)

In the case of an external audit, recommended Real Practice is to appoint an Audit Steering Committee in order to steer the auditor.

---

[1] PR = public relations. The sultans of spin, the masters of perception reality, the shapers of public thinking (if that isn't an oxymoron)

Assess your organisation against *Real ITSM Activities* key practices.   Score 3 for each compliance and 1 for each Bonus.

Total from page 74	
Maintain a Real Risk Register	
Service Desk buffers surges in user activity	
Categorise Requests as PBCK or PBND	
Reduce service levels using SLM	
Log all contacts	
Bonus: Close and reopen Requests as much as possible	
Maintain a Known Idiot database with Runarounds	
Delay service implementation	
Deny service implementation	
Bonus: Have the CEO kill it	
Have a Damage Control function who implement the Three Ds	
Have an EDAB	
Time and resource estimates contain sufficient allowance to permit a normal life	
Schedules are kept full	
Redeployment is resisted	
Progress of projects is closely managed by a PMO	
Keep Away From Sharp Objects	
Mop Up The Mess	
Play With The Car-keys	
Reviewers are briefed	
Data is pre-processed	
Staff are coached	
Reviewers are profiled	
Audit Steering Committee steers external auditors	
Total	

8

Real ITSM Roles

During the introduction of any new change to the way IT works, everyone will insist that new activities are not part of their job.

In order to overcome this, all process frameworks define new roles with new names, so that they can be lumbered on people as an additional responsibility.

Astute managers will make new roles into new headcount. By having new names they can often be smuggled in as new work requiring additional FTEs[1].

---

[1] FTE = Full Time Equivalent. Just as HR actually means people, so FTE actually means staff. But it is easier to treat them like assets (i.e. cattle) if they are known by acronyms.

8.1 Buck Manager

A buck can be defined as any detectable or discernable accountability that has significance for the management of the IT department or their staff or the operation of the department, and evaluation of the impact an accountability might cause to the department.

Real ITSM organisations operate on the principle of functional and hierarchal (horizontal and vertical) buck passing.

For effective functioning of the IT organisation, it is essential that the buck not be allowed to stop, at least not within the department.

The Buck Manager maintains excellent lines of communication with customers, users, executive management, vendors, service providers, government, and anybody else that can potentially be passed the buck.

A Buck Trigger is initiated if a buck appears

- in meeting minutes

- in a report

- in executive management emails or verbal statements

It is the Buck Manager's role to ensure smooth passing of the buck through and out of the IT department (known as "give a flying buck"). This involves

- passing the buck directly

- running interference for anyone else passing it

- identifying and sharing potential buck targets

8.2 *Crisis Manager*

Real ITSM understands that many organisations are experiencing too much volatility to have the time to implement ITIL Change Management process. This is perfectly understandable.   At times of rapid change, resources are not available for Change process implementations. So Real ITSM takes a more pragmatic approach of implementing a Crisis Manager role.

One positive aspect of the role is that crises by definition need no predefined crisis management activities, so implementing the role is quick and cheap.

In times of crisis (and with no change management there will be crises) people become suddenly available. They can be pulled from meetings, training courses, conferences or bed.   Executives pay attention.   Money gets freed up. The Board gets agreeable.

Therefore crises are valuable IT resources that deserve a dedicated Crisis Manager. It is the role of the Crisis Manager to track crises and maximise the consequent benefits for the IT department. This may involve

- revealing a crisis

- communicating the severity to management

- deepening the crisis

- or in some cases precipitating one to meet a serious shortage of resources

The Crisis Manager needs to work closely with Damage Management to ensure incidents are not resolved too quickly before the benefits can be harvested, and with Workload Management to generate something to do for the resulting allocated staff.

8.3 Drek Manager

As discussed in Damage Management, IT departments all crave the peaceful life but no amount to progress management and change management can prevent effluent sometimes combining with air-conditioning. Breaking loose is what all Hell does.

The Real ITSM role responsible for managing the consequences is the Drek[1] Manager.

The Drek Manager has direct responsibility for the Damage Management activity, and for chairing the Damage Advisory Board.

Drek Managers also typically own the Review Management activity as a proactive aspect of their role.

Two roles that should never be assigned to the same person are Crisis Manager and Drek Manager, as the objectives often conflict. The Crisis Manager is often the one who turns the fan on and does the flinging, while the Drek Manager is in charge of wiping up.

**Figure 8-1
Drek Manager**

---

[1] Drek n. *Yiddish* excrement, from *Middle High German* drec

8.3.1 Fire Triage

A key function of the Drek Manager is Fire Triage. Real ITSM organisations have so many metaphorical fires burning (and sometimes actual ones when hardware maintenance falls behind) that they cannot possibly all be addressed, however they may be prioritised and categorised and escalated and assessed and assigned and eventually actually fixed.

So the Drek Manager must apply Fire Triage. This means categorising fires into three groups:

- Those that will burn out on their own. Examples typically include complaining users, requests for reports, incident reviews, and requests for training or manuals.

- Those that cannot be extinguished with any level of available resources. For example: dysfunctional processes, ERP projects, integration of systems from acquired companies, CMDB.

- Those that can be extinguished or diminished.

The first two groups are then ignored, hidden and suppressed.

The third group are prioritised and categorised and escalated and assessed and assigned, in the hope that a few might even be fixed.

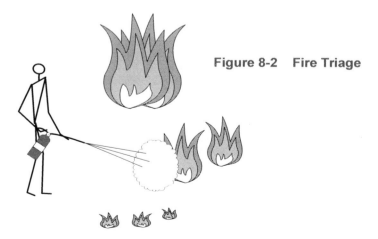

Figure 8-2   Fire Triage

8.4 RACI matrix

A RACI matrix tracks the roles and responsibilities across the various processes. RACI stands for Responsible, Accountable, Consulted, Informed.

	CIO	Operations Manager	Service Delivery Manager	Service Desk Manager	Drek Manager	Buck Manager
Demand Management	C	R	R	R	R	R
Workload Management		R	R	R	R	R
Review Management	I	I	C	R	R	C
High Severity Incidents		I	C	R	I	C
Problem Resolution		C		R		
Event Management		R	I	R		C
Change Management		I	I	R	I	I
Configuration Management				R		
Knowledge Management						

Table 8-1   Real ITSM RACI matrix

Assess your organisation against *Real ITSM Roles* key practices. Score 3 for each compliance and 1 for each Bonus.

Practice	score
Total from page 90	
Maintain excellent lines of communication	
Trigger is initiated if a buck appears	
Ensure smooth passing of the buck through and out of the IT department	
No Change Management process	
Track crises and maximise the consequent benefits for the IT department	
Ensure incidents are not resolved too quickly	
Apply Fire Triage	
Total	

This is your grand total score, your Real Assessment Total Self-assessed (see *RATS*, page 100).

Go to the RITSI website at www.realitsm.com to download these as an assessment spreadsheet of Real Practice and to compare your RATS with that of other Real ITSM sites.

At time of publication, all scores for each key practice were set to 3. The ITSM community can vote on each practice and thereby vary the vote between 1 and 5. Download the spreadsheet from www.realitsm.com to get the latest community-agreed weightings (and so you can vote).

And if auditors or management ask about the status of Real ITSM in your organisation, you can give a RATS.

9
Real ITSM Metrics

Measuring anything brings the risk of accountability, but all superiors need numbers in order to function.

Real ITSM measures the things that matter: the impact on the IT department.

`

9.1 BS

Baseline Satisfaction (BS) is a measure of user satisfaction taken from Service Desk user follow-up surveys. It is important that BS surveys be taken immediately after an incident is resolved. BS surveys can be relied on to return favourable results thanks to three factors:

- The sample population has been pre-filtered to only those who made it far enough to get through to the Service Desk, and then actually have their incident resolved. Anyone who persists that far must have at least a mild bias towards perceiving the Service Desk to be useful

- A high proportion of these people will be happy to just have someone listen and seem to care, whether or not the outcome was beneficial

- A smaller but still majority proportion will have been helped. Get them immediately afterwards and the response will almost invariably be positive. People don't like to seem ungrateful, and the euphoria of a problem gone temporarily erases memories of past wrongs

9.2 FIIK

Failed Inquiries of Information or Knowledge or FIIK is the measure of the number of unfulfilled requests to the IT department for information or advice. This is colloquially known as "404".

FIIK cannot be measured from incident records as nobody in their right mind owns up to responding with a FIIK.

Estimates can be obtained by random sampling using a "secret shopper" to call the Service Desk, or alternatively by multiplying the number of Service Desk calls by 0.75

9.3 FUBAR

Failing Utility Base Analysis Result or FUBAR is the measure of the degradation of a service. Once a service reaches the defined FUBAR threshold, it no longer provides even a trace of useful function and must be shut down for the sake of all involved. This is colloquially known as a "mercy killing".

FUBAR can be measured by

- Number of mentions of the service in staff exit interviews

- Number of articles in the press

- Number of questions asked in parliament/senate

- Total cumulative legal costs

9.4 RATS

The Real Assessment Total Self-assessed or RATS is measured using the assessment spreadsheet from www.realitsm.com or the tables in this book.

Success of Real ITSM implementation is measured in terms of the number of Real ITSM activities and functions implemented, where successful implementation is defined as compliance assessed against Real ITSM.

That is, assess the compliance against the Real ITSM model before implementing Real ITSM, then assess it again after implementing Real ITSM (and again and again). If implementing Real ITSM has increased the RATS, then the Real ITSM project must have been successful.

On no account should any metrics from an organisational perspective (nor any metrics not defined in terms of Real ITSM) be allowed to creep into the post implementation review: these only distort the results.

9.5 SFA

The primary metric of Real ITSM is SFA, or Service Faults Accepted. SFAs are those outages or other service impacts that are acknowledged as being the responsibility of the IT department. SFA should be as low as possible and trending downward.

Service Faults can be attributed to a number of causes that do not contribute to the SFA count, such as:

- external service providers e.g. telco, cabling company, power company, cleaners

- users

- gods, malevolent spirits or ghosts

9.6 SNAFU

Service Norm Actual Functional Usage or SNAFU is a measure of the extent to which the organisation continues to function in the presence of Service Faults. A high SNAFU indicates that organisational reliance on IT is low, which is the preferred situation as this allows IT to maintain existing service levels without noticeable impact. SNAFU can be increased in several ways:

- Ensure the users have paper-based fallback systems

- Encourage localised front-end systems based on Excel or Access for real-time processing of bookings, contact data and other essentials. Users don't mind re-keying data into core IT systems at their convenience, usually after hours.

- Provide flexibility for temp staff to share user logins so that additional staff can easily be brought in to re-enter lost data

- Provide extract facilities so users can maintain their own operational backups

Appendix: Sample Exam Questions

Real sample examinations are designed to scare as many customers as possible into the arms of training providers.

Cost of marking the examinations is minimised by using multiple-choice format. We are confident that candidates who pass a multiple choice examination are demonstrating the skills necessary to produce the kind of proposals, procedures and documentation expected of Real ITSM.

1) On page 49 of *Introduction to Real ITSM* what is the first word on line 10 (counting page headers as lines as well)

   a) the

   b) and

   c) This

   d) By

2) Which of the following is not the opposite of not being unresponding to a user's failure to call the Service Desk?

   a) not calling the user

   b) not failing to call the user

   c) not calling not the user

   d) not the opposite of not calling someone other than the user

3) In developing user requirements for a service design, what is the first step of the process?

   a) Addle the user

   b) Bewilder the user

   c) Confuse the user

   d) Discombobulate the user

4) When an analyst has invested time and money in understanding something new, what will they do next?

   a) Expose the anomalies, follies and inconsistencies to ensure it goes no further

   b) Present an impartial case then await the market's decision

c) Hit the road to generate enough interest to pay back their investment

d) Form an unholy alliance with vendors to drum up some serious money

5) If a CIO is to invest over $1Million with a vendor, what value should he/she expect returned on the investment?

a) a golf shirt

b) several four-figure lunches, with wine

c) a trip to the vendor HQ, two people to the world conference, and invitations to golf

d) a "consultant" job with the vendor later and a world speaking tour

6) The Wright Cycle is named for

a) Orville Wright

b) Wilbur Wright

c) Miss Wright

d) The New Wright

7) For which audience are multi-choice questions best suited?

a) kindergarten

b) primary school

c) trade apprentices

d) gossip magazine sex questionnaires

8) Which of the following is a component of Real ITSM?

    a) Activity

    b) Process

    c) Function

    d) Book

    e) Domain

    f) Area

    g) Section

9) How many Service Desk staff does it take to change a light-bulb?

    a) None. Restoration of service is a Level 1 Support function

    b) None. It is a hardware problem – call the vendor

    c) None. It requires a Change to change

    d) None. They haven't been on the training course

10) How many ~~processes~~ activities are there in Real ITSM?

    a) 7 according to *Introduction to Real ITSM*

    b) 8 according to RITSI

    c) 6.5 according to the Fundament course

    d) All of the above

11) If a business unit attempts to set up their own IT function, what should a Real IT department do?

    a) Explain the risks and inefficiencies of decentralised IT and reason with them

b) Escalate to the executive level to get the idea squashed

c) Do nothing and await the inevitable disaster

d) Source the equipment for them and take a kickback from the vendors

12) What are the "Three Ds"?

a) Doubt, Despair, Decline

b) Donald, Dewey, Daisy

c) Delay, Deny, Duck

d) Divert, Deny, Defend

Answers are on the website at www.realitsm.com/answers

Bibliography

ABC of ICT - An Introduction to the Attitude, Behavior and Culture of ICT, P. Wilkinson and J Schilt, Van Haren 2008, ISBN: 9789087531409

About Core Practice, http://www.corepractice.org/node/55

ITSM From Hell: A Guide to Worst Practices, B. Johnson and P. Wilkinson, Van Haren 2005, ISBN: 9789077212219

ITSM From Hell Based on Not ITIL Version 3, B. Johnson and P. Wilkinson, Van Haren 2008, ISBN: 9789077212004

When 'Best' is Too Good, The IT Skeptic, bITaPlanet 2008, http://www.bitaplanet.com/it_governance/article.php/3688571

Once you have applied Real ITSM and brought yourself some money and time, you might like to read:

COBIT 4.1 Executive Overview and Framework, ITGI 2008, http://www.isaca.org/cobit

FITS pocket guide, Becta 2004, http://www.becta.org.uk/fits

ITAF, a professional practices framework for IT Assurance, ISACA 2008, ISBN 9781604200362

The Official Introduction to the ITIL Service Lifecycle, OGC, TSO 2007, ISBN: 9780113310616

...or not.

Index

5803917R00070

Printed in Great Britain
by Amazon.co.uk, Ltd.,
Marston Gate.